CW01149409

Original title:
Broken Beginnings

Copyright © 2024 Creative Arts Management OÜ
All rights reserved.

Author: Maxwell Donovan
ISBN HARDBACK: 978-9916-90-580-7
ISBN PAPERBACK: 978-9916-90-581-4

Chipped Promises

Once bright dreams now softly fade,
Whispers lost in the masquerade.
What was once whole lies now in shards,
Sparkling shards are all that's left, the guards.

Hopes held tightly in fragile hands,
Turn to dust like ancient sands.
Hollow echoes fill the room,
Chipped promises cast shadows of gloom.

Moments linger on the edge,
Promises broken, a solemn pledge.
Yet in the twilight, hope can rise,
Rebuild the dreams beneath the skies.

Visions Between Shadows

In the creaks of the midnight air,
Visions dance without a care.
Figures flicker, hide, and sway,
Secrets whispered, lost in gray.

The moonlight's glow reveals but faint,
Colors muted, hints of paint.
Shadows merge, realities bend,
In this night, dreams twist and mend.

What lies hidden behind the guise,
Is often seen with closed eyes.
A heartbeats' pulse may guide the way,
Through visions painted in shades of gray.

Mended in the Trying

Fingers worn from the restless night,
Try to stitch up the frayed light.
Each attempt may fall apart,
Yet every flaw holds a piece of heart.

In the weariness of the day,
Hope can bloom in disarray.
Through the struggle, goals refine,
Strength emerges, purely divine.

Threads of doubt may intertwine,
But try again, let courage shine.
With every step, the past will show,
That mended scars can help us grow.

Unraveled Threads

Once neatly woven, now it frays,
Life's fabric shows in splintered ways.
Every cut, a story told,
In the unravel, treasure unfolds.

These threads once bound, now dance alone,
Wavings lost in a world unknown.
But every strand has its own song,
Whispering secrets of where we belong.

To piece together what is torn,
New patterns form in the early morn.
A tapestry of hope and dread,
Stitched with love, where fears are shed.

Frayed Edges

Threads unraveled, stories fade,
Torn pages whisper, memories made.
Time pulls at the seams we sew,
What we hold is all we know.

In the silence, echoes shout,
Fragments lost, but still we shout.
In the shadows, hope still lies,
Frayed edges weave a brand new guise.

Lost in the Re-Assembly

Pieces scattered, hearts in flight,
Searching for a spark of light.
In the chaos, we find grace,
Rebuilding dreams, a soft embrace.

The map is torn, the path unclear,
Yet every step draws us near.
In the fragments, truth will gleam,
Lost in re-assembly, we dream.

A Journey on Unsteady Ground

Tremors shake the path we tread,
Each footstep laid, a hint of dread.
With every stumble, we learn to rise,
Through the fog, we seek the skies.

Uncertainty wraps like a shroud,
Yet in the struggle, we feel proud.
Each misstep writes a tale anew,
On unsteady ground, we find what's true.

When the Past Meets the Future

Time collides in whispers soft,
Echoes linger, dreams aloft.
The past a canvas, the future a brush,
Painting moments in a silent hush.

Footprints etched in golden sands,
History and hope join hands.
When tomorrow calls, we shall respond,
Bridging gaps, of memories fond.

Echoes of Unraveled Dreams

In the quiet of the night,
Whispers linger like dust,
Faded hopes take their flight,
Lost in shadows, they rust.

Figures dance in the dark,
Fractured visions collide,
Each heartbeat a stark mark,
On a journey we bide.

Beneath stars, dreams once bright,
Now flicker and fade slow,
Yet in the depths of night,
A spark may yet still glow.

Fragments of what we sought,
Scattered on winds of time,
Echoes of battles fought,
In the silence, they rhyme.

The Fraying Thread of Tomorrow

A tapestry worn and torn,
Threads of hope come undone,
In the dawn, futures mourn,
   Sewing fears on the run.

Time slips like grains of sand,
Moments lost in the fray,
Visions slip from our hand,
   As we dare not to stay.

What lies ahead, we can't tell,
Yet we clutch to our dreams,
In the shadows we dwell,
Listening to distant screams.

Each stitch bears a story,
Of choices made and missed,
A fabric torn, yet hoary,
In tomorrow's quiet mist.

Collapsed Foundations

Beneath the weight of our days,
Structures crumble and fall,
Whispers echo in haze,
What stands strong, now so small.

Memories sit like dust,
On pillars once so proud,
In the ruins, we trust,
Silence speaks far too loud.

Tremors shake at the core,
Of dreams built on thin air,
What we worked for before,
Now scattered, stripped bare.

From the ashes, we rise,
With the lessons we've learned,
Through the pain and the lies,
Rebirth softly returned.

Whispered Wounds

In the silence, wounds speak clear,
Carved by time, soft yet deep,
Echoes of every lost tear,
Buried secrets we keep.

Behind smiles, shadows lurk,
Stories hidden from view,
In the quiet, they work,
Painting sorrow anew.

Gentle caress of regret,
A touch that leaves its mark,
In the dance of the fret,
We find light in the dark.

Whispers carry the weight,
Of battles fought in our souls,
Healing comes, though it's late,
As we strive to be whole.

The Ruins of a New Horizon

In twilight's embrace, shadows creep,
Whispers of dreams no longer sleep.
Each stone tells tales of battles fought,
Echoes of hopes that time forgot.

Beneath the sky, where secrets lie,
The wind carries words, a quiet sigh.
Fractured hopes in a world so wide,
Yet from the remnants, visions bide.

Nature reclaims what man has lost,
The scars we bear, the heavy cost.
Yet in the ruins, seeds will grow,
From ashes rise, new tales to sow.

Upon the horizon, colors blend,
A promise whispers, the heart will mend.
In every ending, beginnings thrive,
In ruins, the spirit learns to survive.

Born from Cracks

From ancient stone, the life emerges,
Through tiny gaps, the green blood surges.
A push against the weight of stone,
In silence forged, yet never alone.

The world stands still, a watching hush,
Yet life insists with a steadfast rush.
Petals unfurl, breaking the mold,
In fractured earth, the brave are bold.

Roots intertwine in a dance of fate,
Finding their way, though paths seem straight.
Born from despair, in shadows cast,
Each tiny victory, a break from the past.

So let them grow, these dreams of light,
Born from the cracks, they take their flight.
In every struggle, a story starts,
In the heart of chaos, the bloom imparts.

The Sound of Silent Stars

In the deep void where silence reigns,
Stars shimmer softly, free from chains.
Their whispers echo through the night,
Guiding lost souls with gentle light.

In stillness, dreams begin to form,
A tapestry woven, calm and warm.
Each gleam a promise, a tale to share,
In the vastness, love lingers there.

Secrets float on celestial streams,
Carried by hopes and fragile dreams.
The heart listens close, to the unheard,
Finding solace in every word.

Yet in the quiet, the universe sings,
An anthem of peace that softly clings.
Through darkness we find where we belong,
In the sound of stars, we hum our song.

Mistakes in Morning Light

As dawn breaks soft across the sky,
Shadows of doubt begin to fly.
Each choice we made, a lesson learned,\nIn the golden glow, our hearts discerned.

The past may haunt with ghostly grace,
Yet morning's warmth can heal our space.
In every stumble, a chance to rise,
With open hearts, we claim the prize.

Mistakes like freckles, mark our face,
Each a reminder, a traced embrace.
In the light of day, we start anew,
With every sunrise, a clearer view.

So let the morning wash away fears,
In bright reflections, wipe clean our tears.
For in our flaws, perfection lies,
In the dance of shadows, our spirit flies.

Silent Ruins

Whispers in the crumbling stone,
Echoes of a past now gone.
Nature weaves through broken walls,
Silent burdens, time enthralls.

Shadows dance in fading light,
Memories lost, taking flight.
Laughter mingles with the breeze,
Silent ruins, time's decrees.

In the grass, forgotten names,
Silent witness to their games.
Faded portraits, dust and sorrow,
Ghostly tales of yesterdays' morrow.

Stillness reigns where life once thrived,
In these ruins, hopes survived.
Echoes linger, gently hum,
Silent ruins, stillness come.

Ghosts of Yesteryear

Faded faces in the mist,
Memories of a time we kissed.
Whispers of a love once bright,
Dancing in the pale moonlight.

Pictures held in dusty frames,
Fractured dreams and aching claims.
Those who walked with us so near,
Now just shadows, ghosts appear.

Time has cloaked their laughter sweet,
In the corners where we used to meet.
With every sigh, their voices call,
Remnants of the joy and fall.

Echoes of the days gone by,
In our hearts, they never die.
Through the silence, we still hear,
The soft footsteps of yesteryear.

Hopes on Edge

Balancing on a fragile thread,
Wishing dreams could come instead.
Fears and hopes in dizzy dance,
In this life, we take a chance.

Stars align just out of reach,
Lessons life can softly teach.
With each breath, we feel the weight,
Of desires that challenge fate.

Moments fleeting, slipping fast,
Hopes on edge, how long will last?
In the twilight, shadows blend,
Balancing, we dare to bend.

Yet within us, flames still burn,
Through the struggle, we will learn.
Hopes on edge, we carry on,
In every dusk, there's a dawn.

Splintered Dreams

Fractured visions in the night,
Once held close, now out of sight.
Shattered pieces on the floor,
Splintered dreams, we yearn for more.

Winds of change have swept away,
What we hoped would never sway.
In the cracks, the light pours through,
But the visions feel askew.

Glimmers of what could have been,
Haunting echoes deep within.
As we gather broken parts,
Mending wounds within our hearts.

Still we chase the fading gleams,
Through the darkness, cling to dreams.
Splintered, yet we'll find a way,
To rebuild, come what may.

Crumpled Dreams

Once vibrant whispers fade to gray,
Hopeful wishes tucked away.
In shadows where the heart does weep,
Crumpled dreams are buried deep.

Fragments scattered in the breeze,
Fleeting thoughts like autumn leaves.
Tears of dawn in the silent stream,
Reflecting loss in every dream.

Memories stitched with threads of light,
Fading echoes in the night.
Yet a spark may still ignite,
What's lost can be reclaimed in flight.

From ashes rise the dreams once torn,
In the twilight, new paths are born.
Crumpled paper, tales untold,
Renewed visions linger bold.

A Light in the Chasms

In the depths where shadows loom,
Faint glimmers pierce the room.
A flicker dances on the wall,
Promising hope through the pall.

Whispers travel through the void,
Silent echoes, fears destroyed.
Each breath taken, flickers bloom,
Guiding souls through the dark gloom.

Caverns carved with pain and strife,
Yet embers glow with vibrant life.
Hold tight to the luminescence,
A light in chasms, pure existence.

Reach for warmth beyond the deep,
Awaken dreams from slumber's sleep.
In shadows cast by fleeting night,
Find the courage, embrace the light.

Resonance of the Damaged

Voices tremble in the air,
A symphony of muted care.
Notes of sorrow weave through time,
Resonance of hearts that climb.

In silence, stories intertwine,
Life's harsh lessons, a cruel design.
Yet the music, though broken still,
Carries strength within its will.

Chords that fracture, yet align,
In the struggle, beauty shines.
Each scar tells of battles fought,
A melody from pain is wrought.

Listen closely, hear the sound,
The wounded rise from hallowed ground.
Through despair, a new refrain,
Resonance of love, joy, and pain.

The Space Between the Notes

In every pause, a breath of grace,
A quiet moment, a sacred space.
Where silence speaks the loudest truth,
Embracing dreams and echoes of youth.

Starlit skies hold thoughts unseen,
In gentle whispers, worlds convene.
The calm that follows a storm's flight,
A rest where darkness turns to light.

Between the beats, life's rhythm flows,
In the stillness, wisdom grows.
Listen well to what's unsaid,
In empty spaces, futures spread.

Harmony found in every gap,
Life's sweet journey, a wondrous map.
In the silence, hearts will sing,
The space between holds everything.

The Heart's Dissonance

In shadows deep, the echoes play,
A symphony of words once said.
But silence reigns where dreams decay,
And whispers linger, hopes misread.

A tangled web of thoughts collide,
Each note a fragment, lost in time.
The heart is torn, yet cannot hide,
From melodies that climb and climb.

Yet in the chaos, beauty lies,
A fleeting spark in darkest night.
Through dissonance, we find the ties,
That bind our souls in endless flight.

So let the heart embrace the sound,
For even silence has its place.
In every beat, the lost are found,
In dissonance, we seek our grace.

Threads of Dusk

In twilight's loom, the threads entwine,
With hues of amber fading fast.
Each whispered breeze, a soft design,
In night's embrace, where dreams are cast.

The colors blend, a canvas wide,
As stars awaken, shrouded light.
In every heart, a secret tide,
That ebbs and flows to greet the night.

These fragile strands of day and dark,
We weave our stories, bold and true.
In dusk's embrace, we find our spark,
A tapestry of me and you.

So hold the threads, lest they should break,
In twilight's dance, let love abide.
For every moment, dreams we make,
Are woven close, where hopes reside.

Cracked Reflections

In mirrored shards, a face appears,
A fractured view of what was whole.
Each crack reveals our hopes and fears,
The scattered pieces of the soul.

Beneath the gleam, the shadows play,
A testament to battles fought.
In every fragment, light and gray,
A dance of what we've gained and sought.

The cracks, like stories, tell the tale,
Of journeys marked with joy and pain.
Through broken glass, we still prevail,
Each masterpiece, a link, a chain.

So gaze into the depths we hide,
Embrace the flaws that shape our way.
For in these cracks, love will abide,
And guide us through the night and day.

Uncoiled Possibilities

In morning light, a promise stirs,
A ribbon stretched beyond the sky.
The world unfolds, a dance occurs,
With every breath, we dare to fly.

The paths before us twist and turn,
Like streams that flow to distant seas.
In endless dreams, our spirits yearn,
To chase the winds, to ride the breeze.

Each moment whispers of the new,
A canvas waiting for our stroke.
Unraveled threads, a vibrant hue,
With every heartbeat, life awoke.

So let us leap into the vast,
With open hearts and fearless eyes.
For in the now, we find the past,
And in the journey, endless skies.

Strained Calms

The air hangs thick with sighs,
A stillness that belies the storm.
Beneath the surface, tension lies,
Waiting for the world to warm.

In whispered echoes, lost in thought,
The hearts beat slowly, heavy yet light.
In moments wrought with battles fought,
Serenity hides from the night.

Yet in our gaze, a flicker glows,
A spark that dares to break the freeze.
In strained calms, the spirit knows,
That peace can coexist with unease.

So breathe the quiet, feel the pulse,
In every breath, the weight dissolves.
For even in chaos, it convulses,
The calm will mend what pain resolves.

Promises in Pieces

Scattered thoughts on a faded page,
Words once golden now turn to dust.
In the shadow of the silent stage,
Trust crumbles like an ancient rust.

Hold tight to dreams that slip away,
Fingers grasping at the elusive.
Each promise made, a price to pay,
In fragments lost, all seems concursive.

Yet glimmers linger in the night,
Whispers soft like a fragile tune.
Amidst the wreckage, sparks of light,
Remind us that we should be immune.

We gather shards to form anew,
A mosaic built from heartache's grace.
In every piece, a story true,
Promises mend, though time may trace.

Treading Unsteady Waters

Waves rise high, the boat sways low,
Uncertain tides pull at the soul.
With every step, a fear to grow,
Treading waters takes its toll.

The horizon shifts in shadows cast,
Navigating life's hidden rifts.
Though the storm threatens to hold fast,
Hope hangs on as our spirit lifts.

Each splash a reminder of the fight,
Yet strength blossoms in dismay.
In unsteady currents, find the light,
To guide the way when dreams feel grey.

Through tempests fierce, we forge ahead,
With hearts attuned to nature's song.
For every moment filled with dread,
Brings forth the courage to be strong.

The Quiet After the Storm

Leaves whisper low in the muted air,
A lullaby to another day.
The world breathes deep, shedding its care,
In stillness, chaos fades away.

Reflections ripple on glassy streams,
Mirroring skies in soft embrace.
Where once was fury, now flows dreams,
In tranquility, we find our place.

Hearts mend gently under moon's glow,
Each pulse a peace we claim as ours.
In the silence, wisdom will flow,
Rebuilding strength like ancient towers.

So let us wander through this calm,
With every step, a soft refrain.
For in the quiet, we find our balm,
After the storm, we rise again.

Twisted Paths

In shadows deep, the pathways bend,
Whispers call, and hearts descend.
Through the maze, we wander lost,
Choices made, but at what cost?

Branches break, and thorns entwine,
Step by step, we cross the line.
Every twist, a lesson learned,
In the fire of fate, we burned.

Yet in the night, a light will gleam,
A silver thread, a distant dream.
With every turn, we find our way,
And welcome the dawn of a new day.

Ashes of Innocence

Once we played in fields of gold,
Laughter bright and hearts so bold.
Yet time, it steals what we hold dear,
Leaving traces of whispered fear.

In the silence, echoes creep,
Memories fade into the deep.
Ashes falling, sweet songs cease,
In the shadow, we find peace.

Yet from the dust, a spark ignites,
Reminding us of joyful nights.
Through the pain, we start anew,
Rebirth found in every view.

The Fractured Start

In the mirror, cracks appear,
Reflections filled with doubt and fear.
Lost beginnings haunt the mind,
Fragments of what we've left behind.

Each step forward, a hesitant beat,
Searching for solace in the heat.
Paths diverge, the choices spread,
With heavy hearts, we forge ahead.

Yet in the fractures, beauty lies,
In every tear, a chance to rise.
From the wreckage, we create,
A symphony of love, not hate.

Where Dreams Decline

Once bright hopes lit the sky,
Now they flicker, fade, and die.
Whispers of what could have been,
Echo in the silence within.

Stars that shone with vibrant light,
Now are shadows in the night.
Promises made, and then unkept,
In the dark, we silently wept.

Yet still we search for dawn's embrace,
Shattered dreams in time and space.
For even when the light seems gone,
The heart will fight; it carries on.

Shattered Echoes

In the silence where whispers dwell,
Reflections of stories begin to swell.
Fractured moments lost in flight,
Haunting shadows fade with night.

Memories linger, soft and sweet,
In the corners where heartbeats meet.
Voices tremble, yet they stay,
Like ghostly sighs that drift away.

Each echo tells a tale of pain,
A dance of joy, a thread of rain.
In the hush, their weight we bear,
Shattered fragments fill the air.

But in the dark, a spark ignites,
Hope flickers softly, conquering nights.
With every shard that breaks apart,
A new symphony stirs the heart.

Fragments of Dawn

In the cradle of a breaking day,
Light spills forth in a gentle sway.
Colors seep through the tender gray,
As night retreats, shadows give way.

Each ray whispers secrets untold,
Stories of warmth in a world so cold.
Fleeting moments wrapped in gold,
A dance of dreams in the dawn unfolds.

Fragile hues paint the waking sky,
Birds take flight, their hearts soar high.
In every brush, a lullaby,
Fragments sing as the shadows die.

Hope rises with the morning's breath,
Life anew in the face of death.
With every dawn, a chance to mend,
Fragments await to softly blend.

The Wounded Horizon

Across the sky where sorrows bleed,
A canvas stretched with every need.
Scars of time mark the solemn view,
Wounded whispers of skies once blue.

Beneath the weight of a silent plea,
Dreams drift far, lost at sea.
Yet each crest bears a hopeful sigh,
For even wounds can learn to fly.

As daylight fades, shadows crawl,
But within the dusk, we rise and fall.
The horizon aches, but still we see,
Beauty lies in vulnerability.

With every bruise, a lesson learned,
In the heart of darkness, candles burned.
The wounded sky shows us the way,
To love fiercely, come what may.

Unraveled Threads

In the fabric of moments entwined,
Frayed edges whisper what's left behind.
Threads of laughter, threads of pain,
Woven tightly, yet they strain.

Each pull reveals a hidden seam,
Fragments scattered, lost in a dream.
As stories unravel, they weave a path,
Shaping futures from echoes of wrath.

A tapestry rich with colors bold,
Fading threads tell what's been sold.
In each knot, a tale is spun,
Unraveled, yet nowhere to run.

Though tangled knots may cloud the view,
The heart's design is ever true.
In the chaos, find the grace,
Unraveled threads still weave our place.

Half-Imagined Tomorrows

In shadows dancing on the wall,
Dreams whisper secrets, soft and small.
Caught between what is and what could be,
We chase the echoes of a future free.

Hope flickers like a candle's light,
Guiding us through the endless night.
With each heartbeat, we softly sigh,
Yearning for a world where wishes fly.

Yet what is real may slip from grasp,
Like sand that falls through fingers fast.
Still, we linger on the edge of fate,
In half-imagined tomorrows, we await.

From twilight's grasp to dawn's embrace,
We seek the warmth of love's sweet trace.
For in our dreams, we find the way,
To paint the colors of a brand new day.

Pieces of a Fractured Heart

Shattered echoes fill the air,
Fragments glimmer, lost in despair.
Each shard a story, deep and sore,
A tapestry of love and war.

We mend the pieces, thread by thread,
Wounds of the past, a tale still read.
In silence, whispers haunt the night,
Yearning for warmth, for love's soft light.

Yet hope remains, though bruised and scarred,
A spark ignites where dreams are hard.
Through pain, we find our strength anew,
In pieces lies the path we choose.

With every heartbeat, hearts will learn,
From every loss, a flame will burn.
No longer fractured, now we're whole,
A journey forged within the soul.

From Ashes We Rise

When darkness falls and hope seems lost,
The fire within can pay the cost.
From ashes cold, we breathe anew,
Resilience blooms in shades of blue.

With every setback, strength will grow,
A seedling breaking through the snow.
Through storms we face, we will survive,
For in the struggle, we come alive.

The light ahead will guide our way,
Transforming night into the day.
Together, hand in hand we stand,
From ashes rise, a stronger brand.

With courage fierce, we take our flight,
Soaring high into the light.
For in our hearts, a fire burns bright,
From ashes we rise, reclaiming the night.

A Dance on Broken Glass

In twilight's shimmer, shadows play,
A dance of hearts in disarray.
With every step, the shards will fly,
Reflecting dreams that once went by.

We twirl and sway in fragile grace,
Through laughter mingled with the chase.
Though pain may pierce like glass and fears,
We find the rhythm through our tears.

With every turn, the memory clings,
Of love lost midst the shattered wings.
Yet here we are, alive and bold,
In the chaos, stories unfold.

As stars above begin to gleam,
We weave our dance, a fleeting dream.
On broken glass, we find our way,
In the beauty of the night, we stay.

Rusted Dreams

Once bright visions fade away,
Lost in the shadows of decay.
Memories cling like misty dew,
Time erodes all that we knew.

Fragments lie beneath the grime,
Whispers echo, trapped in time.
Hope once shone, now dulled by rust,
Only remnants of our trust.

In the silence, dreams collide,
Seeking solace, trying to hide.
The past may haunt, but still we yearn,
For the fire that once did burn.

But through the haze, a spark remains,
A glimmer fighting through the chains.
Though rust may mar the path ahead,
In every end, new dreams are bred.

A Symphony of Distortion

Soundwaves ripple through the night,
Chaos dances in the light.
Notes collide, a jarring song,
In this world where we belong.

Melodies of joy and pain,
Resonate like falling rain.
Rhythms twist and turn us round,
In the music, we are found.

Voices rise, a choral plea,
Echoing through entropy.
Broken beats, yet hearts still pound,
In this disharmony, we're bound.

A symphony, both raw and real,
In the chaos, we can heal.
Through distortion, we create,
A vibrant world, our shared fate.

Unspoken Disarray

Words unsaid hang in the air,
Silent cries, too much to bear.
Glimpses lost in fearful eyes,
Truths concealed in tangled lies.

Each heartbeat whispers deep regrets,
Echoes of unshared sunsets.
Fractured thoughts and stifled breath,
In this silence, lives are left.

Fingers tremble, hearts confined,
Yearning for the ties that bind.
Yet in the stillness, we remain,
Holding tight to hidden pain.

One day, perhaps, words will flow,
Painting colors to our woe.
In the unspoken, we find grace,
Love can bridge this empty space.

The Aftermath of Renewal

Beneath the ashes, life resumes,
From the dark, a flower blooms.
Softly breaking through the ground,
In the chaos, hope is found.

Seasons change, the cycle turns,
In our hearts, a fire burns.
Scars may tell of battles fought,
Yet within, new strength is sought.

Cleansed by storms, we rise anew,
Facing skies of endless blue.
Lessons learned, like whispered prayers,
Lead us through life's deeper layers.

From the remnants of despair,
Comes a vision, bright and rare.
In the aftermath, we see the light,
Renewed by love, our guiding right.

The Ashes of Tomorrow

In the quiet of the night,
Dreams are softly fading,
Whispers of what could be,
Ashes of hopes cascading.

Stars flicker in the sky,
Lost amidst their sorrow,
We gather all the fragments,
To build the dawn of tomorrow.

Embers of the past remain,
Guiding us through the haze,
With every step we take,
We light our own blaze.

From these ashes we shall rise,
With courage and with grace,
Creating a new vision,
In this sacred space.

Faltering Footsteps

Through the shadows we wander,
Footsteps soft and light,
Guided by the echoes,
In the depth of night.

Each step a word unspoken,
A path we dare to tread,
With the weight of our choices,
In the silence, we're led.

Faltering yet persistent,
We chase the fleeting sound,
In the stillness around us,
New strength can be found.

With every stumble and rise,
We carve our own way clear,
In the journey of our hearts,
We embrace what we fear.

Scraps of Sunrise

Morning breaks with whispers,
Scattered rays of gold,
Painting skies with colors,
New stories to be told.

Each scrap of light that trembles,
Carries warmth and grace,
Turning shadows into hope,
As darkness starts to trace.

We gather all the pieces,
Of a day yet to unfold,
In the heart of the dawn,
A new dream to behold.

With every vivid moment,
We chase the light's embrace,
Finding joy in fragments,
In this sacred space.

Songs of the Fallen

In the meadow of memories,
Where whispers linger still,
Songs of those who've faded,
Echo through the hill.

Each note a soft reminder,
Of laughter and of pain,
In every fleeting moment,
A love that will remain.

They dance upon the breezes,
With a beauty so profound,
Stories of the brave hearts,
In their voices, they're found.

From the ashes of the past,
We honor every name,
In the songs of the fallen,
Their spirits we reclaim.

Dismantled Aspirations

In a room filled with dust, they lay,
Dreams once bright, now gray,
The plans we penned in brighter days,
Scattered hopes in disarray.

Each piece tells a tale of loss,
At what point did we count the cost?
Whispers linger in the air,
Of futures lost, of silent despair.

With every sigh, another break,
The voice of promise starts to quake,
A vision lost, a path unclear,
Yet still we wander, gripped by fear.

But even in the wreckage bright,
A spark will flicker in the night,
From fragments, we might recompose,
New dreams to nurture, new seeds to sow.

Echoes from the Past

In the halls where laughter thrived,
Shadows dance as memories arrived,
Every corner speaks a name,
Of whispered hopes, and whispered shame.

Beneath the weight of aged regret,
The heart recalls, it won't forget,
Footsteps echo, soft and slow,
Times of joy, times of woe.

Photographs in a dusty frame,
Eyes that sparkle like a flame,
Stories linger in hushed tones,
Remnants of love in broken homes.

Yet in the silence, strength is found,
Resilience blooms on hallowed ground,
The past may haunt, but it can heal,
In echoes, the heart learns to feel.

The Weight of First Chances

With trembling hands, we reach for fate,
The doors swing wide, we hesitate,
A heartbeat quickens in the still,
With every choice, we shape our will.

Promises whispered in the dark,
A first ignite, a hopeful spark,
Each step a mixture of fear and chance,
In delicate rhythm, we begin to dance.

But oh, the weight of paths untaken,
The dreams we shaped, and those forsaken,
A burden borne with every risk,
In the chaos, our hearts still lisp.

Yet courage grows with every fall,
From every stumble, we stand tall,
First chances may slip from our hands,
But still, we rise, and forge our plans.

Shards of a New Chapter

From broken pages, stories rise,
In shattered pieces, new hope lies,
A chapter closed with lessons learned,
For every bridge, a fire burned.

Fragments glimmer in the light,
A vision forms, sharp and bright,
Each shard a token of what's true,
In every ending, something new.

Breathe in the air of change so sweet,
Life reawakens with every beat,
As paths converge, the past recedes,
In unity, we plant new seeds.

With light on horizons we once sought,
In the rubble, dreams are wrought,
A tale begins, with pages crumpled,
Yet in the chaos, spirits rumpled.

Splintered Paths

In the silence of the night,
Footsteps echo, lost in flight.
Choices made, yet paths divide,
Wandering hearts with nowhere to hide.

Whispers of the past resound,
In tangled roots, the truth is found.
Fragments of a once-clear way,
Now a maze where shadows play.

Each turn a chance to redefine,
To embrace fate, to seek, align.
Yet still we tread on broken ground,
Searching for the love we've found.

Hope flickers like a distant star,
Guiding us, no matter how far.
In splintered paths, we take our stand,
Together, united hand in hand.

Ashes of a New Start

From the embers, dreams arise,
Flickering flames beneath the skies.
Old ways burn, a cleansing fire,
Igniting hearts with newfound desire.

The past may linger with its weight,
But ashes pave the path to fate.
Out of darkness, hope is spun,
A tapestry, the journey begun.

With every breath, we rise anew,
Embracing change, a brighter view.
The phoenix flies, reborn in light,
From ashes, strength ignites the night.

Together we forge, hands intertwined,
Creating lives that brightly shine.
In the silence, futures sing,
From ashes, we take to the wing.

Fragments of Hope

In the cracks of a weary soul,
Shattered dreams begin to stroll.
A whisper here, a glimmer there,
Pieces scattered, yet still we care.

The winds may howl, the storms may rage,
Yet hope remains, a sacred page.
In fragments lost, we find our way,
A path revealed with each new day.

With every scar, a tale unfolds,
Strength forged in stories told.
In the rubble, love will bloom,
Turning shadows into room.

Hold tight to dreams, though torn apart,
For in the fragments, lives a heart.
In every piece, a spark ignites,
Fragments of hope, our guiding lights.

Tattered Dreams

Once vibrant hopes, now worn and frayed,
Tattered edges, memories laid.
Yet in the fading, beauty shows,
A mosaic of what love bestows.

In quiet corners, secrets seep,
Through threads of time, the heart will weep.
Yet every tear holds stories dear,
Woven patterns, laughter, and fear.

Though dreams may wear, they still ignite,
A flicker of warmth in the coldest night.
In every snag, a lesson learned,
Through tattered dreams, our spirits yearn.

So stitch together fragments bright,
Revive the hope, embrace the light.
For even tattered dreams can soar,
Transforming hearts forevermore.

Wounded Wishes

In the quiet of the night,
A whisper formed in pain,
Wishes lost in shadows,
Carried by the rain.

Hopes that once were glowing,
Now flicker dim and low,
Wounded hearts still dreaming,
Waiting for the glow.

Promises like ribbons,
Fraying in the breeze,
Holding on to fragments,
Yearning for release.

Yet through the broken silence,
A spark begins to rise,
Wounded wishes mending,
Reaching for the skies.

Faded Tracks

On a road once lively,
Footsteps fade away,
Whispers of the journey,
Lost in yesterday.

Memories like shadows,
Dance along the line,
Faded tracks where heartbeats,
Once did intertwine.

Time has worn the moments,
Leaving tales to tell,
Paths that led to nowhere,
Echo in the shell.

Yet through the desolation,
Hope glimmers anew,
Faded tracks still guiding,
To places bold and true.

Ashen Futures

In the haze of twilight,
Dreams grow faint and cold,
Ashen futures linger,
Stories left untold.

Stars that once were shining,
Now drowned in muted light,
Whispers of tomorrow,
Fade into the night.

But within the embers,
A spark begins to glow,
Ashen futures rising,
From ashes down below.

Hope ignites with fervor,
Breathes life in every soul,
Though futures may be ashen,
They can still be whole.

Battered Blossoms

In the storms of nature,
Blossoms bend and break,
Battered by the darkness,
Yet they still awake.

Petals torn and faded,
Colors lost in strife,
Battered blossoms blooming,
In the dance of life.

Through the winds of chaos,
Resilience takes its hold,
Finding strength in softness,
While the tales unfold.

In the warmth of springtime,
Beauty finds a way,
Battered blossoms rising,
Welcome every day.

Torn Pages

In a book where stories fade,
Whispers echo, softly laid.
Memories linger, shadows twine,
Torn pages blur the sacred line.

Fingers trace the faded words,
In silence, the heart is stirred.
Lost chapters roam, seeking light,
In the dark, they find their fight.

Fragments worn from time's embrace,
Every tear reveals a place.
In chaos, beauty starts to bloom,
Among the remnants of the gloom.

Yet still we seek a tale untold,
In every whisper, hearts unfold.
The stories lie both raw and pure,
In torn pages, we endure.

Missteps in Moonlight

Underneath the silver glow,
Footsteps falter, quiet and slow.
Shadows dance in soft twilight,
Misdirections of the night.

Each stumble holds a whispered fate,
Wandering paths we contemplate.
In the stillness, dreams collide,
Missteps guide us, hearts abide.

Stars above, they watch and sigh,
As wishes drift into the sky.
For every wrong turn, there's a sign,
In moonlight's grace, we intertwine.

So let us walk where shadows weave,
In missteps, we dare believe.
With every fall, a chance to rise,
In the dance of night, we find our ties.

A Canvas of Imperfections

Brush strokes bold, colors bleed,
A tapestry of human need.
In every flaw, a story spins,
A canvas where the heart begins.

Crimson hues and azure skies,
Layers deep with hidden sighs.
Each crack and scratch, a tale to tell,
Of love, of loss, where shadows dwell.

The beauty lies in what's not right,
In every tear, a glimpse of light.
With open hands, we paint our scars,
In imperfections, we find our stars.

So let the colors merge and fade,
In every stroke, the price is paid.
A masterpiece, uniquely ours,
In a world adorned with broken hours.

The Color of Fractures

In the glass of shattered dreams,
Light bends through fractured beams.
A prism shows what's left behind,
In every crack, the heart resigned.

Faded hues of what was whole,
Reflect the echoes of the soul.
In brokenness, new shades arise,
Crafting beauty from the lies.

The art of scars, in shades of grey,
Tells a story in a twisted way.
A palette rich with depth and pain,
In every fracture, hope remains.

So let us find the strength to see,
The vibrant hues that set us free.
In a world of cracks, we will discover,
The color of fractures, like no other.

When Hopes Collide

In twilight's grasp, we stand apart,
Two dreams entwined, yet worlds apart.
Hopes rise like smoke in the evening air,
A fragile dance of love and despair.

Blue skies now dim with shadows bold,
Stories untold, and futures sold.
With every glance, a whispered plea,
When hopes collide, what will we be?

The echoes linger, a haunting sound,
Lost in the void where light is found.
Fates intertwine, then fray at the seams,
In the silence, we chase fading dreams.

But through the wreckage, a spark ignites,
Resilience blooms in the darkest nights.
Together we rise, from ashes we fly,
When hopes collide, we learn to defy.

Scattered Beginnings

Each dawn unfolds like a page anew,
Scattered whispers of dreams pursued.
In the gardens of time, we plant our seeds,
Nurturing hopes, tending to needs.

Footsteps echo on paths unknown,
Winding trails of heart and bone.
With every breath, a chance to reignite,
Scattered beginnings take to flight.

In the tapestry of moments we weave,
Stories of joy, and hearts that grieve.
Together we wander, hand in hand,
Searching for magic in the shifting sand.

Let the winds carry us where we dare,
To the uncharted, the bold, the rare.
As stars align in the vast expanse,
Scattered beginnings spark a dance.

Dissonant Harmonies

In a world where silence screams,
Dissonant harmonies shatter dreams.
Notes collide in a chaotic symphony,
A clash of shadows, a lost epiphany.

Fingers on strings, a heart out of tune,
As twilight descends, under the moon.
Melodies weave through the fabric of night,
Each discordant note a flickering light.

Voices mingle in a restless breeze,
Trying to find what brings us peace.
Yet in the chaos, where sorrows bind,
Dissonant harmonies fuse heart and mind.

But as night wanes and dawn draws near,
Hope resounds, a song we hear.
In every clash, connections arise,
Dissonant harmonies lead to the skies.

Reflections in the Ruin

Amidst the stone where shadows lay,
Reflections linger, a ghostly sway.
In whispered winds, lost tales abide,
Echoes of laughter, where dreams collide.

Through the cracks of time, we search for light,
In ruins of memory, faded but bright.
Each crevice tells of love and pain,
Reflections in the ruin, a bittersweet gain.

Grass grows wild where footsteps fade,
Lost in the echoes of choices made.
In the silence, a story unfolds,
Reflections in the ruin, where time beholds.

Yet from the ashes, new life will rise,
Hope like a phoenix will touch the skies.
In every fragment, a beauty grows,
Reflections in the ruin, the heart still knows.

Faded First Steps

In a field of whispers, we once danced,
Little feet tracing dreams in the sand.
Echoes of laughter in sun-kissed light,
Faded memories drift in the night.

Each stumble a lesson, each fall a chance,
To rise again stronger, start a new dance.
With hearts wide open, we dared to explore,
Faded first steps, but we longed for more.

Through the haze of time, we search for grace,
Chasing the shadows, lost in the chase.
Yet within our hearts, a glow still remains,
Faded first steps, forever ingrained.

The journey stretches, paths intertwine,
With every heartbeat, our spirits align.
Though footsteps may fade, the stories stay bright,
In the dawn of our dreams, we ignite the night.

The Cracked Canvas

Silent strokes upon the aged wood,
Colors bleed where dreams once stood.
A painter's lament in each weary line,
The cracked canvas speaks, though the heart may pine.

Once vibrant visions, now shades of gray,
Forgotten frames, as hope drifts away.
Yet in every fracture, beauty's embrace,
The cracked canvas holds time's gentle trace.

With brush in hand, I revive the past,
Layer by layer, shadows are cast.
Finding the light in the depths of despair,
The cracked canvas, a story laid bare.

In every blemish, a tale to be told,
Fragments of courage in hues bold.
Though the surface bears scars of the fight,
The cracked canvas still dances in light.

Shards of Promise

Scattered pieces across the floor,
Shards of promise, we can explore.
Each fragment glimmers, a tale to unfold,
In the heart of the broken, new stories told.

With hands outstretched, we gather the light,
Turning the darkness into something bright.
A mosaic of dreams, both fragile and bold,
Shards of promise, a treasure to hold.

Through storms of doubt, we learn to mend,
Finding our strength as we learn to bend.
Though shattered, our spirits rise like the sun,
Shards of promise, our journey's begun.

In every fissure, a spark still gleams,
Together we'll craft all our wildest dreams.
Embracing the chaos, our hearts align,
Shards of promise, forever we shine.

Misguided Ventures

With maps uncharted, we set our course,
Misguided ventures fueled by our force.
Through tangled woods and rivers wide,
We chase the horizon, side by side.

Each twist and turn, a lesson in fate,
Finding our way, although it feels late.
In the heart of the fray, we stumble and fall,
Misguided ventures, we conquer it all.

Yet beneath the stars, we find our way,
Guided by dreams, come what may.
Though paths may wander, our spirits stay true,
Misguided ventures lead me to you.

In laughter we leap, in silence we grow,
Through trials and triumphs, love starts to show.
Together we wander, forever entwined,
Misguided ventures, our hearts aligned.

When Seeds Falter

In the soil, hope lies low,
Waiting for the sun's warm glow.
Yet the whispers of the night,
Breathe doubts that stay out of sight.

Gentle rains may come and go,
Yet the seeds refuse to grow.
Dreams buried in barren grounds,
Echo softly, make no sounds.

But the heart knows how to yearn,
Through the pain, the twists, the turns.
With patience, life will find a way,
To break the dark and greet the day.

From each fissure, light will stream,
A testament to every dream.
Seeds of courage, seeds of grace,
Will rise again, find their place.

The Divided Journey

Paths that cross and paths that part,
Each step holds a fragile heart.
Between the choices lies the fate,
Of dreams we nurture, or abate.

Winding roads and twisting trails,
Through the storms and sunlight gales.
Voices call from far and near,
Whispering hopes, laced with fear.

With every turn, a lesson learned,
In varied ways, our souls are burned.
Yet through shadows, we still tread,
Seeking light where angels wed.

The journey's long; the journey's wide,
With every heartache, love's our guide.
In every tear and every smile,
We find our strength to go each mile.

Unfinished Stories

In the margins, dreams await,
Silent tales of love and fate.
Words unspoken, lives untold,
Yearning hearts break from the mold.

Each chapter starts with hope anew,
Yet often folds like morning dew.
Pages crumple, yet we strive,
To keep the fire of dreams alive.

With every pause, we seek the end,
Hoping time will help us mend.
Storylines twist, collide, and fade,
Yet in our hearts, the ink cascades.

Blank spaces hold potential bright,
For every dawn, a fresh insight.
With open arms, we write our part,
In unfinished tales of the heart.

Shadows of a New Path

In the twilight, shadows dance,
Hiding secrets in their prance.
A new path calls with whispers low,
Yet uncertainty steals the glow.

Footprints linger, tales of yore,
Echoes of what came before.
Yet the heart, it knows no chain,
Through the dark, we map the plain.

With every step, a chance to soar,
To embrace the unknown and explore.
For in shadows lie the dreams we seek,
A silent truth, though voices weak.

So to the light, we dare to flee,
Along the path where we can be.
In shadows cast, we find our light,
In every ending, new beginnings ignite.

The Tattered Map

Worn edges speak of roads once trod,
A journey traced beneath the stars.
Faded lines and inked dreams lost,
Whispers of adventures, past memoirs.

Each crease holds a forgotten tale,
Of mountains high and valleys deep.
Guided by hope, yet faced with doubt,
In every spot, secrets still sleep.

Rain has blurred what once was clear,
Navigating through life's wild sways.
Yet seekers hold the treasure near,
In every twist, a path still lays.

Through shadows cast by distant peaks,
Brave hearts venture on this map of old.
For even if the way seems bleak,
The journey's worth more than gold.

Rusted Foundations

In the stillness beneath the grime,
Walls whisper tales of days gone by.
Structures stand, with stories entwined,
Yet dreams decay as time drifts by.

Rusty beams hold weight of the past,
Each creak a reminder of life lived bold.
What once was vibrant, now holds fast,
To memories of whispers, now untold.

Nature weaves through cracks and stones,
Birthing new life in the grip of decay.
Yet underneath the old, the bones,
Of a future lost, in disarray.

To build anew, we must discard,
The weight of what no longer stands.
In every grit, we bury hard,
The chances missed by timid hands.

Abandoned Aspirations

Dreams once bright, now gathering dust,
Visions of hope slip through the seams.
Silent echoes haunt the trust,
Of paths imagined, fading dreams.

In the corners, shadows blend,
With unfulfilled plans that lay in wait.
Time bends soft, though hearts contend,
To chase the future, defy the fate.

With every sunset, a chance remains,
To reclaim what's lost in the haze.
Though longing lingers, like autumn rains,
We rise again to face new days.

Let not the silence bind the soul,
For in the stillness, seeds do grow.
Abandoned dreams can still be whole,
If nurtured gently, they will glow.

Echoes of Yesterday

On dusty roads where footsteps fade,
Each whisper of wind recalls the past.
Fleeting moments, memories made,
In the echo of laughter, shadows cast.

Glimmers of light from old lanterns shine,
Through crevices of time, they weave.
Stories linger, like aged wine,
In the heart's cellar, we still believe.

Voices rise from the depths of night,
Songs of sorrow and joy combine.
With every star, a spark of light,
Guiding us home through the divine.

As dusk embraces the dying day,
We cherish the map of where we've been.
For echoes of yesterday gently sway,
Reminding us of the lives we've seen.

Once Wholeness, Now Frayed

Once we danced in twilight's grace,
Laughter echoed, every space.
Now the threads begin to fray,
Memories scatter, drift away.

Fragments of joy, lost in the night,
Whispers linger, fading light.
Trust that held, now just a thread,
Our once-bright hearts, heavy with dread.

Time has etched its lines of care,
Promises fade into thin air.
Yet in the shadows, glimmers stay,
Hope peeks through every disarray.

Though we're broken, not alone,
In these pieces, love has grown.
From the frayed, we'll weave anew,
Finding strength in what we rue.

The Eclipsed Dawn.

Night has whispered, shadows creep,
The world rests in silent sleep.
Yet promises of light remain,
In the darkness, hope's refrain.

Stars above, like scattered dreams,
Guide us through those shadowed beams.
But as the skies begin to part,
An eclipsed dawn stirs the heart.

Colors fade, the sun retreats,
Yet in the gloom, courage beats.
We wait for light, the break of day,
In this pause, we find our way.

For every dark, a chance to rise,
Beyond the veil, a bright surprise.
Through eclipses, life's dance goes on,
In every dusk, awaits a dawn.

Fractured First Steps

Tiny feet on fragile ground,
Every movement, echoes sound.
Unsteady heart, yet dreams in tow,
Learning life as time will flow.

Fallen leaves mark paths once clear,
Every stumble, learning near.
With each step, the world expands,
A fragile courage in small hands.

Hands that reach, and hearts that yearn,
In this dance, we twist and turn.
Though the path is never straight,
In each fracture, we create fate.

Among the slips, the fright, the fall,
There's a whisper, a beckoning call.
Fractured first steps lead to the vast,
Every moment holds treasures cast.

Shattered Dawn.

Morning breaks with heavy sighs,
Sunrise cloaked in muted cries.
Shadows linger where hope had sworn,
In the light, our dreams are worn.

Fragments of light through cracks that tear,
Whispers of what once was fair.
Yet in the shards, a beauty gleams,
Rebuilding life from broken dreams.

We gather pieces, stitch by thread,
From the wreckage, softly tread.
Each new dawn, though bruised and raw,
Offers strength to mend, a law.

Though shattered, we find ways to stand,
With every break, we understand.
In the dawn that struggles to rise,
We glimpse the light beyond the lies.

The Scarred Threshold

Beneath the arch of shadows cast,
Old echoes call, forgotten past.
A door with dents, its stories told,
In silence keeps, what time enfold.

Every scratch, a tale to share,
Of moments lost, of weight and care.
With trembling hands, I push and pry,
To find the truth that dares to lie.

The winds that whistle, sharp and cold,
Know all the secrets that I've sold.
The threshold stands, both bold and shy,
Yet beckons me, to jump or fly.

I step across, the world anew,
A scarred threshold, yet it's true.
For every wound, a chance to heal,
And face the dawn, with strength to feel.

Lost in the Prelude

Beneath the stars, a whisper glows,
In twilight's grasp, where silence flows.
A melody, soft yet profound,
In every heartbeat, lost and found.

The moment lingers, time suspends,
A fleeting dream, where daylight bends.
Captured breath, caught in the air,
The shadowed notes, a weight to bear.

Each sigh is woven, dusk's embrace,
While echoes dance in empty space.
A prelude calls to those who wait,
In twilight's waltz, we contemplate.

Yet here I stand, between the lines,
A riddle wrapped in subtle signs.
And though I'm lost, the path is clear,
To find the music woven near.

Tides of Disarray

In restless waves, the ocean sighs,
Each tide a tale, a truth that lies.
A chaos spun, of shells and foam,
In disarray, we still call home.

The horizon blurs, the sky ignites,
In swirling doubts, we seek the lights.
Yet with each swell, I feel the pull,
Of hidden depths, both wild and full.

Footprints washed, like fleeting dreams,
Yet still I wander, or so it seems.
In chaos found, we weave our song,
In disarray, we still belong.

The moon commands, the stars align,
In tangled waters, love's design.
So let us drift, through ebb and flow,
In tides of life, we learn to grow.

The Fissured Launch

From cracks in earth, the fire grows,
A fissured launch, where passion flows.
With trembling ground, the sparks ignite,
In trembling hearts, the urge to fight.

The sky expands with every leap,
A promise held in whispers deep.
A journey stirs, the time is near,
To soar above, to face the fear.

Yet here I stand, on edges worn,
A fissured path, yet hope reborn.
In every step, the courage swells,
To chase the dreams, where freedom dwells.

The launch awaits, with breathless grace,
I take a chance, to find my place.
And through the cracks, I find my way,
In fissured launch, I greet the day.

Fragments of a New Day

Morning light spills through the trees,
A soft whisper dances on the breeze.
Hope awakens with the dawn's embrace,
New beginnings in every space.

Birds chirp sweet melodies around,
Nature's symphony is joyfully found.
The world stirs from its gentle sleep,
In this moment, promises we keep.

Colors bloom in vibrant hues,
Each petal tells a story anew.
Take a breath, let worries stray,
Embrace the fragments of a new day.

As shadows fade and dreams take flight,
We craft our paths in morning light.
Together we rise, hand in hand,
In the fragments of this hopeful land.

Whispers of Another Chance

In quiet corners, secrets lie,
Soft murmurings that pass us by.
Echoes of dreams once held so dear,
Whispers beckon, inviting us near.

A second look at faded trails,
All the stories that love entails.
If time can bend to heal the heart,
Then here's our chance to restart.

Raindrops fall like gentle sighs,
Each one carries a sweet reprise.
With every drop, a fresh design,
Promises made, and hopes align.

So listen closely, don't let go,
In the stillness, new seeds will grow.
This is the time for us to dance,
In the whispers of another chance.

Crackling Embers

The fire's glow in the dark of night,
Dances softly, flickers bright.
Each crackle tells a tale long spun,
In this warmth, we are all one.

Ashes flutter, memories rise,
A fragile beauty beneath the skies.
Like dreams that simmer, then ignite,
Hearts are kindled in the night.

Gathered close, we share our fears,
With laughter, love dispels the tears.
As embers fade, still we remain,
In the warmth, we'll rise again.

A spark ignites when hope feels low,
Through crackling embers, light will flow.
Together we weave, our stories blend,
In the twilight, we'll find our mend.

The Beauty in Imperfection

Cracks in pottery, stories unfold,
Each flaw reveals a heart of gold.
The beauty lies in what's not right,
In every shadow, there's a light.

A crooked line, a lopsided smile,
In these details, we find our style.
Embrace the chaos, let it show,
Life's true essence starts to glow.

Dusty corners hold a charm,
In the rawness, we feel the warmth.
Nature thrives in its wild state,
Imperfections do not dictate fate.

So let us cherish every flaw,
In the depth, we'll find our draw.
In the imperfect, we come alive,
Finding beauty where hopes survive.

A Prelude to the Unforeseen

In whispers of dawn, secrets awake,
The breeze carries tales yet to break.
Each step towards the unknown path,
An echo of fears, a dance with wrath.

Clouds hover softly, painting the skies,
With shadows of dreams that quietly rise.
Beneath the surface, a storm may brew,
While silence holds promise of something new.

Time ticks slowly, a moment in wait,
For the turn of a page, the opening gate.
What lies beyond, the heart can't foresee,
Yet hope lingers on, wild and free.

A sudden turn, the world rearranges,
With every heartbeat, life subtly exchanges.
In this prelude, our spirits unite,
Ready to embrace the unfathomed light.

Tangled Destinies

In shadows of fate, our paths entwine,
Threads woven tight, a delicate line.
Every glance shared, a choice we create,
Unraveling stories as we navigate.

Beyond the borders of time and space,
Two souls entwined in an intricate lace.
With laughter and tears, we forge anew,
The beauty in chaos, our journey true.

In moments of silence, our spirits collide,
Finding the strength in the rising tide.
Together we wander, through sun and storm,
In tangled destinies, our hearts stay warm.

With every heartbeat, our fate holds fast,
A melody sung, through future and past.
Forever connected, we brave what may,
Tangled destinies guide our way.

The Shattered Canvas

Upon a canvas, colors bleed,
Fragments of dreams, wild to succeed.
Every brushstroke, a tale untold,
In the chaos of art, beauty unfolds.

Crimson despair meets gold of hope,
In the shattered pieces, we learn to cope.
From the wreckage, new visions arise,
Painting our truth with passionate cries.

Each drop of ink, a moment of grace,
Life's palette mingles in every space.
Through broken hues, we find our way,
Creating a masterpiece, day by day.

Amidst the debris, the heart takes flight,
A testament of courage, shining bright.
On this shattered canvas, we stand tall,
In art's embrace, we reclaim it all.

Flickers of Light Amidst Shadows

In the depths of night, whispers ignite,
Flickers of hope, breaking the fright.
Stars scatter gently, a shimmering dance,
Guiding lost souls with a fleeting glance.

Among the shadows, courage begins,
A spark in the darkness, where light quietly wins.
Each glowing ember, a story to share,
Illuminating hearts, banishing despair.

In every heartbeat, a promise remains,
That even through trials, joy can sustain.
The shadows may linger, but they cannot stay,
For light finds a way to guide our stray.

Embrace the night, let the moments unfold,
In the flickers of light, our dreams are bold.
With every dawn, the shadows retreat,
Replaced by the warmth of hope's steady beat.

Milton Keynes UK
Ingram Content Group UK Ltd.
UKHW022222251124
451566UK00006B/85